Ben and Pop Star

story by Jeremy Strong
illustrated by Steve Smallman

Ben and Tessa like to visit their grandparents.

They are called Big G and Little G.

Big G likes to cook.

"You are so messy," says Little G.
Big G laughs. "I know!"

One day Big G said to Ben,
"What are you doing at school?"

"I am learning to play the guitar," said Ben.

"I played the guitar once," said Big G. "I still have it. Come on."
They went upstairs.

There was a little door to the loft.
Big G opened the door and a ladder came out.

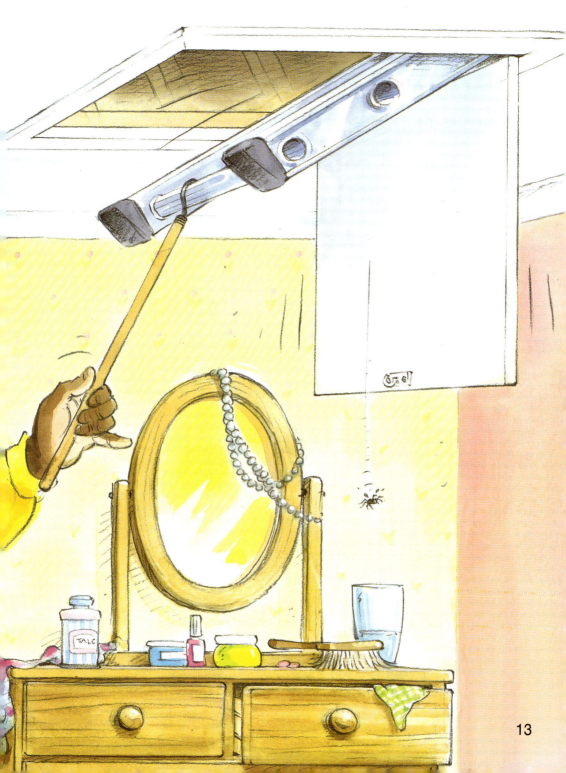

It was dark.
Big G had a torch.
"There it is!" he said.
There were cobwebs on the guitar case.

When they went downstairs
Little G pulled a face.
"You two are so messy!" she said.
"We know!" they said.

Big G opened the case.
"An electric guitar!" shouted Ben.

"I can still play," said Big G.
"I could be a pop star."

Twang!
Big G began to play and sing.
Little G put her fingers in her ears.
"Stop! Stop!" she said.

Everyone laughed.

Ben said, "You are no good as a pop star but you **are** a good cook."